Take up
Golf

Take up Sport

Titles in this series currently available or shortly to be published:

Take up Golf

Principal contributor:
Jim Gregson
Jim Gregson has written several books on golf,
and is a regular contributor to a leading golf magazine.

SPRINGFIELD BOOKS LIMITED

Copyright © Springfield Books Limited and White Line Press 1989

ISBN 0 947655 59 X

First published 1989 by
Springfield Books Limited
Springfield House, Norman Road, Denby Dale, Huddersfield
HD8 8TH

Reprinted 1991

Edited, designed and produced by
White Line Press
60 Bradford Road, Stanningley, Leeds LS28 6EF

Editors: Noel Whittall and Philip Gardner
Design: Krystyna Hewitt
Diagrams: Chris Oxlade

Printed and bound in Hong Kong

Photographic credits
Cover photograph: © Allsport
Jim Gregson: pages 17, 18, 20, 23, 24, 26, 27, 28, 29, 42, 44, 45, 49, 50, 58
Supersport: page 8
Noel Whittall: pages 6, 10, 11, 13, 15, 30, 32, 37, 46, 51, 53, 55, 56, 57, 60, 61, 62

Acknowledgements
Our thanks to Gerrards Cross and Rawdon Golf Clubs; to the golfers featured in most of the photographs: Richard Pheasant, Nicholas Booth, Iain Lawson and Rita Shaw; and to Jonathan Pitts, teaching professional at Rawdon.

Contents

Driving off towards the distant target.

The challenge of golf

Most people who take up golf have played other ball games, and by comparison golf looks easy: there is no opponent to produce an unplayable ball, send a demon service, or rob you with a tackle. In golf you approach a dead ball in your own time and select a club; when quite ready, you move unhurriedly to the shot, swing easily, and dispatch the ball effortlessly towards a distant target. We all know that this is true because we've seen the professionals on television play like this time after time!

Why then does golf suddenly become so difficult when you come to try it for yourself? Most of the problems arise because you have to hit a very small ball with the almost equally small surface of a club. Herein lies the challenge and the frustration of this most beguiling of games. You have to hit the ball accurately, and the greater the distance you wish to hit the ball, the more accurately you have to bring together club and ball. As the full golf swing involves the use of all the major muscles of the body, you need to co-ordinate many movements in a complex way. Golf is a game with tiny margins of error.

Undoubtedly, you will go through times when golf will be very frustrating, but stick with it — in the end you will find that it really is great fun, and well worth all the effort.

A fast-growing sport

The origins of golf are the subject of some debate, although it is certain that a game which resembled today's was played in Scotland in Elizabethan times. It took the next few centuries for the game to become really popular in Britain, but its progress has gathered speed, and the last hundred years have seen a golfing boom. It is now played by millions of men and women throughout the world, and the top championship players have become familiar names in every continent.

The rules of golf

The rules of golf are many and complicated — you may think unnecessarily so sometimes, but they are designed to take into account every conceivable situation which can arise on the course. Keep an up-to-date copy of the rules in your golf-bag whenever you are playing — while they may sometimes seem to be a formidable hindrance, they might also help you to get out of a difficult situation! We do not have room in this book to list all the rules, but some of the more widely used and important ones will be introduced where appropriate.

The modern rules of golf are controlled by the sport's joint world governing bodies, the Royal and Ancient Golf Club at St Andrews in Scotland and the United States Golf Association. Your club or pro shop should have copies available, but if you have any difficulty, contact your national golf association (see pages 63–64).

There's no age-limit in golf, and the game appeals equally to men and women.

2

Equipment and clothing

Clubs

There are three different types of golf club: *irons*, *woods* and *putters*. Let's take a look at what these are and then see what selection of clubs you will need as a beginner.

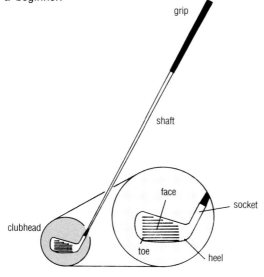

Figure 1 The parts of a club

Irons

Irons have a clubhead forged from metal. There are quite a few irons — the full set includes a 1-iron through to a 9-iron, a pitching wedge (sometimes called a 10-iron), and a sand wedge. The lower the number, the straighter the face of the club, the longer the shaft, and the further a ball hit with the club will travel. The irons are often divided into three groups:

- long irons (1, 2, 3 and 4)
- middle irons (5, 6 and 7)
- short irons (8, 9 and the two wedges)

Woods

Woods are clubs with a clubhead fashioned from a block of laminated wood. There are five different woods — 1-wood through to 5-wood, the 1-wood normally being called the driver. As with the irons, a lower number means that the face of the club is more upright and its shaft is longer.

Putter

The putter has an upright face for hitting the ball along the ground. Although the function of every putter is the same, it is here that club design is most varied.

Choosing your clubs

Don't be put off by the number of clubs listed above — you don't need all of them by any means! The max-

imim number that the rules allow you to carry is four-teen, and for a novice there can be advantages in be-ginning with half that number. When you are struggling to lay clubhead on ball with any consistency, greater choice only means more problems!

You should acquire a "half set" of irons. This means that you have either the odd or the even numbers — 3, 5, 7, 9 or 4, 6, 8, pitching wedge. The very long irons (1 and 2) are difficult to use and are best left to the experts.

You can manage with a single wood (a 3-wood), but will probably enjoy having two. Most golfers are "macho" enough to want to whack away with a driver, but as the driver is the club which allows the smallest margin for error, you will probably do better with a 3- and a 5-wood to start with. The 5-wood is certainly the easiest club to use if you are trying for a reasonably long shot from the fairway. If you really must have a driver, buy a 3- or 4-wood as well.

With the addition of a putter, you will have a set of clubs which will enable you not only to take up golf, but also to progress to a high level of skill. Many fine players never carry any more than this selection of clubs.

◄ *Apart from the putter at the front, the angle of the clubface increases progressively from the driver (1-wood) to the pitching wedge.*

A typical "half set" of clubs. The woods have the longest shafts, followed by the low-numbered irons.

Ladies' and men's clubs are different — those for ladies are about an inch shorter, and slightly lighter. Also remember that if you are left-handed, you need a left-handed set of clubs!

Finally, when you play a bad shot, look for the fault in yourself, not your clubs: golfers are generally the worst of all sportspeople for blaming their equipment for their own failings!

Golf balls

There are two types of golf ball: "wound" and "solid". Wound balls were the normal type until a few years ago; they are made by winding thin elastic thread tightly around a small core, and covering the resulting hard rubber ball with a plastic jacket. The solid balls are a relatively new development. As the name suggests, they are moulded from solid plastic. The governing bodies of golf have very strict rules about how far the ball should travel when hit with a specified force, so differences between balls are slight. The best ball for a beginner is the solid ball, which flies just a little further than the wound ball. More importantly, it is much more durable in the face of ill-treatment: you must expect to hit many less-than-perfect shots as you seek the distant heaven of golfing excellence!

All golf balls have to comply with international regulations, and from 1 January 1990 these require them to be not less than 1.68 inches (42.7 mm) in diameter. Beware of "cut price" offers of balls which conform to the old specification of 1.62 inches (41.1 mm).

Clothing

There are no restrictions on what you wear for golf, although most clubs require you to play in fairly smart clothes ("no denims" is the normal rule). Make sure your clothes allow you room to swing freely. Once the game has gripped you strongly enough to lure you out into weather most sensible people would avoid, you will need to think about a set of waterproofs and an umbrella.

Shoes
You will need a comfortable pair of golf shoes. You must decide for yourself whether you prefer the traditional shoes, with spikes in the soles, or the newer shoes with "pimpled" soles, which some golfers find are more comfortable and still give a reasonable grip. Many golfers have a pair of both: spikes for wet or winter conditions and pimples for drier weather.

Other equipment

With the addition of a golf bag, tee-pegs, a pencil for recording the scores on the scorecard, a scrap of towel to wipe your clubs (which you should do after every shot) and a tiny fork for repairing marks where the ball has bounced, you are ready for the fray.

When first buying equipment, keep your outlay to the minimum until you are sure that this infuriating game is worth your full commitment.

Many players find that a broad-wheeled trolley is a worthwhile accessory.

Learning the game

Tuition

One of the aims of this book is to keep the instruction simple — if you can concentrate on the essentials of the golf swing, you will improve rapidly. As your fascination with the game grows, you will be drawn to much larger books of instruction. Some of them make the essentially simple business of swinging a golf club far more complicated than is helpful, and none of them can check whether you are interpreting and implementing their well-meant advice. The person to give you "on the spot" guidance and to look for faults which you cannot see for yourself is a *teaching professional.*

You need not pay for individual attention at the outset. There are many coaching opportunities available for beginners. Most local authorities now run beginners' classes, taught by local Professional Golfers' Association (PGA) professionals, and some local golf courses, particularly municipal ones, run their own group courses for beginners. These courses represent the cheapest form of expert guidance for most people starting the game. They will also put you in touch with a group of like-minded people of about your standard, so that you can encourage each other's successes and commiserate with each other's failures.

Practice

Tuition from a teaching professional will be of little use if you do not practise what you have learned. A good professional will concentrate on one or two important aspects of the swing in each lesson; once you have understood and reproduced these once or twice during that lesson, it is essential to go away and practise them. Ideally, this should be on a proper practice ground at a club. By all means play on the course as well, but bear in mind that the practice ground is the only place where you can repeat the same shot time after time, and that is what builds consistency, one of the most difficult elements of the game.

If you do not have access to a practice ground, you can swing away at lightweight plastic practice balls in the garden. Put an old doormat down to hit them from: many lawns have been ruined by the efforts of novice golfers!

Practising on competition days
If you are going to play in a strokeplay competition (see chapter 6 for an explanation of strokeplay and other forms of play), you are not allowed to practise on the course on the day of the competition. There is no such restriction for matchplay.

A valuable lesson from a teaching professional

Building a golf swing

The secret of successful golf is to build a swing which is both *effective* and *consistent*. The basics of your swing should be the same whatever club you have in your hand; the adjustments you need for different shots are minor, and stem from common sense rather than any complicated mystique. Let's look in turn at the four aspects of every golf shot: grip, stance, backswing and downswing.

Grip

The forces involved in driving a golf ball down the fairway are considerable. Your club will weigh only a few ounces, yet as you swing it at full speed to hit the ball, a pull down on the shaft of over one hundred pounds is produced. When the clubhead meets the ball, it will be travelling at around 100 miles an hour (50 m/s) and the impact force will be more than a tonne. Your only contact with these formidable forces is through your hands — hence the importance of a sound grip.

It is essential that your hands operate as a *single unit* — in most bad grips, one hand dominates the other, producing various unwanted effects when the clubhead hits the ball. When right-handed players (we will assume that you are right-handed — left-handed people should simply swap left and right where they appear throughout the book) play a shot, they swing with the back of the left hand leading. This means that you are simultaneously playing a backhand shot with the left hand and a forehand shot with the right. An efficient grip will make sure that your hands work together.

Most golfers use the Vardon grip (named after its originator, Harry Vardon), and it's the one we recommend for you — you can see how to form it in the photographic sequence on pages 17–18. A good grip will probably feel unnatural at first, but eventually your hands will fall into place so automatically that you will wonder how you could ever have held the club differently!

With the clubhead resting on the ground, pointing away from you, place the club diagonally across your open left hand so that it lies in the crook of the first finger.

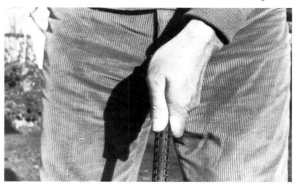

Close your left hand, so that the thumb rests just on the right-hand side of the shaft.

Now place your right hand below your left, with its little finger overlapping the first finger of your left hand. The shaft should rest along the roots of the other three fingers.

Close your right hand so that your left thumb fits snugly into your right palm and your right thumb is on the left side of the shaft.

Wrap the little finger of your right hand around the first finger of your left hand. That's it — the complete Vardon grip.

Some players prefer to interlock these fingers instead (it's still a Vardon grip) — try both ways and use whichever feels most comfortable for you.

Checking your grip

It is very easy for your hands to twist around the handle of the club, either forwards or backwards, and this will have an adverse effect on your swing. With the clubhead resting on the ground in front of you, check that:

● the Vs formed by the thumbs and forefingers of both hands are pointing somewhere between your chin and your right shoulder;

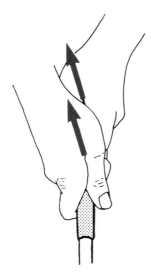

Figure 2 The grip showing the Vs

● you can see no more than the first two knuckles of your left hand.

Finally, remember that you grip with your *fingers* — to be precise, the last three fingers of the left hand and the first two of the right; if the palm of the right hand comes into play, you will lose all the feel and accuracy of the shot.

Stance

You need to develop a regular routine when you set yourself up to play each shot.

Firstly, stand behind your ball, look towards the target, and work out which way you want to hit the ball — this establishes the *line of the shot*. Note a point on this imaginary line a few feet (a metre or so) in front of the ball, so that you can judge the line afterwards simply by looking at it, rather than by looking up at the target again.

Assess the shot from behind the ball. Choose your target, and "see" the shot in your mind's eye.

Move round beside the ball, and, with your feet together, place the clubhead behind the ball, with its front edge square-on to the line of the shot. The distance you stand from the ball will depend on the length of the club you are using — you will be further away when using the longer irons and woods.

Now move your feet apart into a comfortable posture. They should be an equal distance in front of and behind the ball for an iron shot, but put a little extra weight onto your right foot: this will move your head slightly to the rear of the ball. Bend forward from the waist, keeping your back straight, and let your arms hang from your shoulders, so that you are ready for a swing that is comfortable but in which your arms stay close to your body.

Left: *With your feet together, place the clubhead squarely behind the ball.* **Right:** *Move your feet into position; your head should be just behind the ball.*

This setting-up procedure may seem complicated at first, but after a time your body will fall naturally into a good stance. This is the first stage in what professionals call "grooving a swing". All this should take you a few seconds only — it does not need to take longer.

Check your alignment

Shoulders, hips and feet should all be parallel to the line of the shot. A useful trick here is to imagine yourself on a railway track: one rail follows the ball-to-target line; you stand on the other, with shoulders, hips and feet all lined up parallel to the first rail. Shoulders are the most difficult to align, because you cannot easily check them yourself. Unfortunately, they are also the most important element to get right — you can hit good golf shots on occasions, sometimes deliberately, with your feet off-line, but you will never manage to hit a full shot well if your shoulders are off-line. The only effective way of making sure your shoulders are aligned correctly is to ask a friend to check for you.

Addressing the ball

When you have taken your stance and the club has touched the ground behind the ball, you have *addressed* the ball, and you are now in the *address position* or *at the address*. You can be penalised if the ball moves once you have addressed it, even if you do not make a stroke (see page 43).

The backswing

Now you have taken your stance, let's look at the final stage of preparation for the shot — the *backswing*.

Why do teachers and manuals give this process such detailed attention? Well, the backswing has two purposes: to *build power*, and to get your body into a position from which you can hit in the right *direction*. Get your backswing right and you greatly increase your chances of hitting the ball far and straight.

Building power

To build power, you turn your shoulders while resisting with your hips. Your shoulders should turn through about 90 degrees, and your hips through about 45 degrees. These angles are just a guide — you don't really have to think in such precise terms. Just turn your shoulders as far as they will go (the feeling is of turning your back on the target), and your hips, even though they are resisting, will have to move to let your shoulders turn fully. Your right knee should remain roughly where it is, and virtually all your weight will have transferred onto it by the end of the backswing. Your left knee should move slightly back towards your right knee — not towards the ball.

Throughout the backswing, you should keep your left arm as straight as you comfortably can, but not stiff. At the top of the swing, your right elbow should be pointing at the ground. Don't make a conscious attempt to "cock" your wrists near the top of the backswing — the momentum of the clubhead will do it for you.

If you have turned correctly, you should not be able to hold the position at the top of the backswing for longer than a second or two.

The plane of the swing

Power is useless without accuracy. To hit the ball straight, you need to swing the club back and down again in such a way that it stays in the same *swing plane* all the time. The angle of the swing plane will vary a little according to the club you are using and your height.

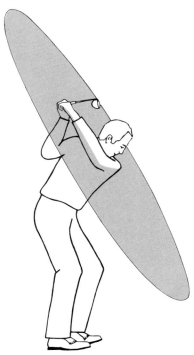

Figure 3 The coloured circle indicates the swing plane; its angle will vary according to your height and to the club you are using.

Begin the backswing with shoulders, hips and feet parallel to the line of the shot.

Keep the left arm straight as the shoulders turn and the hips resist. Notice that the head has not moved — keeping your head still is vital.

The top of the backswing — the club is pointing towards the target, and the "spring" is ready to uncoil.

If you make a complete swing in the correct plane, the shaft of the club will be pointing at the target when you have reached the top of your backswing. If the stroke you are making does not need a full swing, the plane should still be just the same, so that, if you were to continue the backswing, the shaft would again point at the target.

Get a friend to check the shaft direction at the top of your backswing for you — frequently. If your backswing is out of the correct plane, the clubface is unlikely to hit the ball square-on when you swing it back down again.

Slicing and hooking
If the clubface hits the ball at a slight angle instead of square-on, sidespin is imparted to the ball, causing a *slice* (the ball swings away to the right) or a *hook* (the ball swings away to the left).

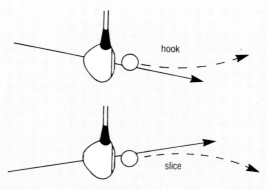

Figure 4 Slicing and hooking

Left: *The club is pointing left of the target. This will pull the clubhead across the ball, causing a* slice.
Right: *With the club pointing right of target, you are likely to* hook *the ball.*

Summing up

Two images will be helpful when you are learning the backswing:

● You should feel as though you are pivoting around a steel pole that begins at the back of your head and runs to the ground through your trunk.

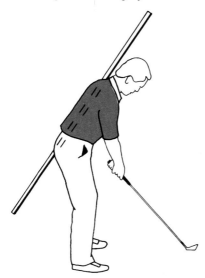

Figure 5 The imaginary steel pole

● At the top of your backswing, you should feel like a coiled spring, ready to be released at the ball.

Finally, do not "cheat" on one aspect of the swing to correct a fault in another. For example, do not relax your left-hand grip or bend your left arm to get the club shaft pointing at the target at the top of the backswing — you will lose control of the club and never regain it. Instead, get the club into its proper position by turning your shoulders.

The downswing

Any healthy person who is prepared to take pains can grip a club, adopt a stance and swing the club back — irrespective of his or her skill at games. But now we come to the *downswing*, which is where flair and timing tell: you have to combine a number of different body movements at speed.

By the top of the backswing, you should have generated power and charted direction; the trick of the downswing is to release the power without losing the direction.

Co-ordination is all important: your hands and arms must swing the club into the ball in time with the return of your hips and shoulders to the address position. If you think of the downswing as a series of separate movements, you are heading for disaster.

Always keep in mind one piece of golfing advice — "swing the club*head*". If you swing the clubhead as easily as you can, you will get the other elements of the downswing, such as transferring your weight from right to left foot, correct automatically.

1

2

3

Photographs on pages 26 and 27:

1 *The downswing starts here — weight on the right foot, shoulders fully turned and club pointing towards the hole.*

2 *The arms pull the club down and the weight begins to move onto the left foot.*

3 *Nearly back to the address position. Note that the hands are leading the club slightly.*

4 *The ball is away: the eyes are still watching the point of impact as the right arm straightens through the ball.*

5 *A full, high and balanced follow-through.*

Fighting the tendency to slice

It is no good swinging the club back in the correct plane if you don't bring it down in that same plane. The object is to hit the ball so that it goes straight, but ninety per cent of golfers have a natural tendency to slice the ball so that it spins off to the right of the target. This is generally caused by an optical illusion which gives the impression that the clubhead is going to be just too far away from the ball as the club comes round from behind you. Most players feel that they are bringing the clubhead down "on the outside" (further away from the body than when it went back), and try to compensate by pulling the clubhead across the ball — hence the slice.

If you can ignore the illusion, you should not have a problem, but if the slice persists, play the shot as if you are attempting to come into the back of the ball very slightly "from the inside" (closer to your body than on the backswing), rather than absolutely straight. At first the feeling will be of trying to hit the ball a few degrees to the right of the target — just where it is tending to go without any help. Don't be put off by this: because you will actually be hitting square at last, the ball will go straight.

The only reason shots fly to the right or left of the line — assuming no interference from the wind — is that the club face has not met the ball squarely.

***Photographs on pages 28 and 29 — the downswing
seen from a different angle:***

1 *Left arm straight and eye on the ball throughout.*

2 *Shoulders and hips begin to swing around that "steel
pole" running through the spine.*

3 *The correct downswing brings the club "from the
inside".*

4 *The hips have cleared out of the way, and the clubhead
has struck down and through. Note how the golfer's head
remains still until the shoulders pull it up in the follow-
through.*

Points to remember in the downswing

Bear these points in mind if you want to get this key
movement right:

● Complete your backswing before you start down
again. This might sound obvious, but failure to do so
is the most common cause of disastrous "snatching"
at the ball.

● Swing as slowly as you can. Then you stand every
chance of keeping the clubhead in the correct swing
plane. Don't try to hit the ball too hard — you will hit
the ball further by hitting it *better*, not harder.

● With all clubs except the driver, the clubhead should
reach the bottom of its swing just *beyond* the position
of the ball. Unlike a cricket bat or tennis racket, where
you lift the ball by angling the surface, golf clubs have
angled surfaces built in. One of the many paradoxes of
the game is that you swing *down* to get the ball *up*.

● Hit *through*, not *at*, the ball. Make sure you keep the
clubhead moving not just up to the ball, but past it.
Concentrate especially on the few inches beyond the
ball to give yourself every chance of striking it solidly
and squarely.

- Give some attention to your follow-through: it is a fairly good guide to what has happened before. If you end your follow-through off-balance, you were probably off-balance much earlier in the swing. You cannot hit good shots consistently if you are off-balance at any stage.

- Remember that throughout the swing — both when going back and coming down — you are pivoting around that steel pole running through your spine.

A classic follow-through from the drive: Nicholas has not looked up until the ball is well on its way, and his club completes the swing fully. Don't be afraid to let the clubhead come right round like this.

On the golf course

Having learned the basics of an effective swing, let's go out and familiarise ourselves with the various features of the golf course.

The holes

In golf, *hole* has two distinct meanings:

● It is the actual hole in the green into which the ball must go. The position of the hole on the green will be changed from time to time so that a particular part of the surface does not become too worn.

● It is the entire strip of land between the tee and the green, including the fairway, the rough and all the bunkers and other hazards. You will hear expressions such as "an easy hole", "an uphill hole" and "a difficult hole". Not all the words used by frustrated golfers to indicate the degree of difficulty are printable here!

Most golf courses have eighteen holes, and a *round* of golf consists of playing each of them once. Some courses have only nine holes, in which case you play the course twice to make up your round. The round is divided into two halves: the *outward* or *front* nine and the *inward* or *back* nine. The holes are referred to by number (from one to eighteen), and each will usually have a name as well. The distance from the teeing ground to the green is the length of a hole. On a typical course, this will range between about 150 yards and 550 yards (140–500 m). Not all holes are straight — they often have a bend in them to avoid natural obstacles.

Before you play each round, make sure you get a *scorecard*. This gives you details of each hole on the course, provides space for writing down the scores (more about scoring in chapter 6), and gives a list of "local rules". It will also give the *par* of each hole.

31

This overall view of a course shows many of the elements that you are likely to encounter during a round: markers for the teeing grounds can be clearly seen in the foreground, and the light sand of a couple of bunkers makes them stand out. The trees in the background — which count as part of the course — make sure there is no shortage of problems around these holes!

Par

Par is the "standard" number of shots which you should take to finish a hole. It is based simply on the length of the hole:

Par	Men		Ladies	
	yards	metres	yards	metres
3	0–250	0–230	0–200	0–180
4	251–475	231–435	201–400	181–365
5	476+	436+	401+	366+

Par-four holes are the most common — a typical golf course might have four par-threes, ten par-fours and four par-fives. The overall par for a course is simply the addition of all the pars for the holes — 72 for our typical course.

Terms of the course

Let's look at a typical golf hole and explain some of the terms that you will come across. We will also look at some of the rules which relate to the layout and conditions of the course.

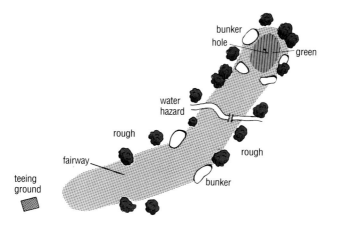

Figure 6 A typical hole

The teeing ground
The teeing ground is the area at the start of each hole from which you hit your first or *tee shot*. There are usually separate teeing grounds for men, for ladies and for competition play. There are two markers on the teeing ground which define the area in which your ball must be placed (see Figure 7).

Teeing up is the expression used for placing the ball on a *tee-peg* before hitting it towards the hole. You are only allowed to use tee-pegs within the area of the tee-ing ground.

Figure 7 The teeing ground is a rectangular area two club-lengths deep

Fairway

The area of fairly close-cut grass between the teeing ground and the green is called the *fairway*. It does not necessarily start at the teeing ground; par-three holes, where you are expected to reach the green with your tee shot, have no fairway at all.

Rough

The area of longer grass, bushes, heather, etc. along the sides of the fairway is called the *rough*.

Out of bounds

On some holes, there are areas off the fairway which are *out of bounds*. An example might be the area on the other side of a fence at the edge of the golf course. There is a penalty for hitting your ball out of bounds (see page 50). The "local rules" section of your scorecard should give a list of areas on the course which are out of bounds.

Hazards

These are *bunkers* (hollows with sand in the bottom) and *water hazards* (streams, lakes, drainage ditches, etc.).

As a general rule, if your ball is in a bunker, you have to play it where it lies (see chapter 7). In a water hazard this may not be possible, so you are allowed to drop the ball, or its replacement, outside the hazard. If you do this, you accept a penalty of one stroke, and the ball has to be dropped somewhere on an extension of the imaginary line passing through the flag and the point where the ball entered the water hazard. Naturally, you are not allowed to drop it any nearer to the hole than the hazard.

The green

The green is the area of very close-cut grass in which the hole is situated. Around the green there is often an area of slightly longer grass called the *apron*.

Ground under repair (GUR)

Some areas of the course, for example a very worn piece of turf, may be marked as ground under repair. You can move your ball from ground under repair if it lands there. There are rules for the way the ball has to be moved: see *dropping the ball*, page 51.

Casual water

Casual water is water which lies on the ground as a result of heavy rain or flooding. It does not include water in hazards. You are allowed to move your ball out of casual water without penalty.

6

Scoring

There are quite a few different types of competition in golf, and the scoring depends on which one you play. Each has one thing in common — the number of shots it takes you to get the ball from the tee into the hole is counted. Your score on each hole is then the number of shots which you actually hit plus the number of *penalty* strokes you collect along the way.

Special names are given to scores, depending on how different they are from the par of the hole:

Par The term *par* also refers to a score equal to the par value of the hole.

Birdie This is a score of one shot less than par (e.g. a four on a par-five).

Eagle Two less than par (e.g. a "hole-in-one" on a par-three).

Albatross Three less than par (this can normally only be done by scoring a two on a par-five).

Bogey A score of one more than par (e.g. a five on a par-four). A *double bogey* is two over par, and so on.

Forms of play

There are too many different types of competition for them all to be explained here, but we will look at the two basic types of play and how they are scored.

Matchplay
In matchplay, you play against an opponent to try to win each hole. If you take fewer shots than your opponent, you win the hole. If you both take the same number of shots, then the hole is *halved*. The score in the match is simply a measure of how many more holes you have won than your opponent. An example follows on page 36:

Hole	Result	Your score
1	lose	one down
2	win	level
3	win	one up
4	halved	one up
5	win	two up

etc. (let's assume you gain two more holes along the way...)

15	halved	four up

At this point the match is over, since there are only three more holes to play and, even if you lost them all, you would still be one up at the end of the eighteenth. You are four up with three to play and are said to have won by "four and three".

There are quite a few different formats within matchplay: *singles* is played between two players; in *foursomes*, two pairs play each other, the members of a pair hitting the same ball alternately; in *four-ball* there are also two pairs, but each player has a ball and the better score of the pair on each hole is counted against the better score of the other pair. *Stableford* and *bogey* competitions are further variations, where the players' scores are calculated relative to a fixed score at each hole. The fixed score is usually the hole's par.

Make sure you understand the rules of a particular competition before you set foot on the course! Experienced golfers will always explain the details to a newcomer.

Strokeplay

Strokeplay is the simplest form of golf competition: you simply add up your scores at each hole to give you an overall score for a round. Strokeplay is more demanding than matchplay, since if you get a disastrously high score on one hole it can ruin what might otherwise have been a good overall score, whereas the loss of a hole in matchplay can be made up at the next hole. The winner of a strokeplay competition is the player with the lowest score at the end of the last hole. You will often hear strokeplay referred to as *medal* play.

Handicapping

Golf differs from most other sports in that you can play against any other golfer, no matter what standard, and still enjoy a close competition. This is because all golfers have a *handicap* — which is really a measure of how good they are. As an example, a player with a handicap of 20 would be expected to play a round of strokeplay in about 20 shots more than the overall par for the course. The minimum handicap is zero – the handicap of a "scratch golfer". The maximum handicap awarded (and probably what you will have as a beginner) is 28 for men and 36 for women.

In strokeplay, you deduct your handicap from your total score for the round to give you a *nett* score. In matchplay, if your handicap is more than your opponent's, you will "receive" a shot on some holes, as indicated on the scorecard (see page 39). For example, if you score a five, it might become a *nett* four, and four would be the score that counts.

If you want to play in competitions, you will need to have an official handicap. This is awarded by the handicapping committee of a golf club, who work it out from your most recent scores.

Standard scratch score (SSS)

This is the total number of strokes in which a scratch golfer might be expected to play a course. It is based on the total length and difficulty of the course rather than the pars of the individual holes. This system is used in calculating handicaps so that a player from a club with a relatively easy course receives the same handicap as a player of the same standard from a club with a difficult course. The SSS can now vary from day to day, reflecting the performances of the field in a particular strokeplay competition.

The handicap system allows players with widely differing levels of skill to compete against each other on an equal basis.

The scorecard

The rules require you to use a scorecard for stroke-play. There is no such requirement for matchplay, but it is not a bad idea to use a scorecard anyway, as it gives you a record of the match.

Your scorecard gives you quite a lot of information. Usually the *local rules* are stated, telling you such things as which areas are out of bounds or are to be treated as permanent water hazards.

There will also be a number of columns with data about the holes, as well as the essential blank column where your scores are put. You don't fill in your own score: a "marker" is appointed to do this. The marker is usually a fellow-competitor.

Typically, the column headings may be:

● Hole
● Length
● Par
● Stroke index
● Player's score
● Win +, Loss -, Half 0

Hole is simply the number of the hole. Golf courses are normally played according to the sequence of hole numbering, although sometimes it is permissible to play the "second nine" first.

Length is the length of the hole in yards or metres.

Par is the par rating of the hole. It gives you an indication of the length of the hole (see table on page 32).

STANNING
STANDARD

Hole	Length (yards)	Par	Stroke index	Score	Win + Lose - Half 0	Hole	Length (yards)	Par	Stroke index	Score	Win Lose Half
1	357	4	6			10	409	4	2		
2	369	4	8			11	318	4	10		
3	339	4	11			12	334	4	3		
4	144	3	13			13	333	4	12		
5	394	4	5			14	310	4	7		
6	103	3	17			15	154	3	14		
7	474	4	1			16	261	4	18		
8	253	4	16			17	176	3	9		
9	505	5	4			18	122	3	15		
	2938	*35*					*2417*	*33*			

TOTAL SCORE [   ]
HANDICAP [   ]
NETT SCORE: [   ]

Player's signature ....   Marker's signature ....

Figure 8 A typical scorecard

Stroke index Each hole bears a number, from 1 to 18, which is to show you where you deduct the extra strokes to which your handicap may entitle you during matchplay. The system works like this: imagine that you have a handicap of 20 and your opponent has one of only 15; the *difference* in your handicaps is 5. This difference is multiplied by an *allowance* (normally 0.75 for singles matchplay). In this case 5 x 0.75 = 3.75, which is rounded up to 4. Therefore you are entitled to an extra stroke at the holes with a stroke index number from 1 to 4.

Player's score It should not be too hard to work out that this is where the marker notes the number of strokes you took for the hole. However, in matchplay, you do not always hole the ball — your opponent can beat you before you even reach the green — so this column may remain empty.

Win +, Loss –, Half 0 Use this column in matchplay to show whether you have won, lost or halved the hole; always reckon this from your nett score, which takes into account any strokes credited according to your handicap.

There may also be columns headed *LGU* and *LGU par*. These refer to the rating of the hole when played from the ladies' tees (see page 33). Most clubs, however, have separate cards for ladies.

The scorecard may also mention the *standard scratch score* (SSS). This can be a guide to the overall severity of the course. If the SSS is much less than the total par score, the course will be fairly easy.

OLF CLUB
H SCORE 66

LOCAL RULES

, Stones may be removed from any part of the course. If the ball is oved in the process it must be replaced in the same position.

, Players must always replace divots.

, Out of bounds: (i) outside the boundary limits of the course; (ii) e clubhouse and the paths around it; (iii) the area demarcated by hite posts on the sixth hole; (iv) the area between the banks of the iver Stanning.

, Water hazards include all permanent ditches and drains.

, Ground under repair includes tractor tyre marks.

, A ball coming to rest on a putting green not belonging to the hole eing played must be lifted and dropped back off the green, but not earer to the hole.

7

Aspects of the game

Using the different clubs

Fairway woods

These are the 3-, 4- and 5-woods. They have fairly long handles, so, as with the driver, your swing should be wide and flat. Position yourself in relation to the ball so that you hit it at, or just before, the bottom of your swing, and *sweep* the ball away — don't hit *at* it. Concentrate on rhythm and balance: these are important factors in all golf shots, and the woods are the best clubs to help you develop them.

Long irons

Most amateur golfers find that their long irons (3 and 4) are the most difficult clubs to use, and will often use a 5-wood in preference to a 3-iron. However, if you think of long-iron shots as sweeping shots, like shots with a wood, you will find them easier to master. This technique will allow you a greater margin for error, because it keeps the clubhead close to the ground for quite a long time at the bottom of the swing, as well as preventing you from chopping into the ball.

Many of the difficulties beginners experience with these rather unforgiving clubs arise from trying to hit the ball too hard. Discipline yourself to swing unhurriedly (this is surprisingly difficult!) and hit with a long iron no harder than you would with a short iron — you will find that you hit the ball not only better, but also further.

Short irons

Accuracy is paramount when playing a shot with short irons. Normally you will be aiming at a green, trying to achieve both the right line and the required length.

It is more important than ever now to make sure your shoulders are exactly on the intended line of your shot, and that your shoulders and arms swing along that line very accurately. To ensure this, you may find it useful to stand a little "open" (see panel). This will cut down your body movement in the swing and allow your shoulders and arms to follow the line of the shot without your hips getting in the way. Swing easily, and hit the ball and *then* the ground, taking a divot. Resist the temptation to move your head to inspect the results of the shot until you are sure the ball is away.

Taking an "open" stance
Although you should normally line your feet up with the line of the shot, on some occasions it helps to move your left foot back a few inches. This will make your feet align to the left of the target, which creates an "open" stance. Your shoulders should still be along the line of the shot.

Figure 9 Foot positions for an "open" stance

Types of shot

Driving

Driving is the term used for hitting the ball off the teeing ground. At most holes the club you use is a wood — often the driver.

The driver is the longest club, and so you stand the furthest distance away from the ball to use it. You have to use a fairly wide swing, so stand with your feet slightly more than shoulder-width apart to give yourself a solid base. All this is simple logic: if you try it with a club you will find that you cannot do otherwise if you are to keep the swing you have worked at.

The driver has a fairly upright face, and so the ball will need to be positioned opposite your left heel if the driver is to make the ball rise. This means that when the clubhead meets the ball, it will have passed the bottom of its swing and will be going up again. You also need to *tee high*: the tee-peg is not pressed in very far, so that the ball is well off the ground. As a general rule, when the ball is addressed by the driver, about half of it should be above the face of the club.

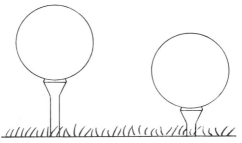

Figure 10 Tee the ball high for a driver, lower for irons and other woods

Sweep the ball away, with a wide, unhurried swing. If you rush the shot the clubhead will trail behind the rest of your swing and cut across the ball, causing a slice.

Wound up for the big drive! The ball is opposite the left heel and the shoulders have turned fully. Notice that the hands are high and the grip is firm.

> **If your ball moves...**
> If your ball moves after you have addressed it and
> before you swing, you are given a penalty of one
> stroke. However, this rule does not apply on the
> teeing ground, where, if your ball falls off its tee peg,
> even if you knock it off yourself when you address it,
> you can replace it without a penalty.

Another of golf's problems will quickly become apparent
when you use the driver: the further you hit the ball, the
straighter you have to hit it! Simple geometry dictates
that an imperfectly-struck ball will end up further off-
course after two hundred yards than after sixty. Unfortunately, this problem is amplified because the driver is
the most difficult club with which to hit the ball straight.

One plus point here: though the driver is the most
difficult club to use with accuracy, you are normally aiming at the biggest target on the course — the fairway,
which may be sixty yards or more wide. So do not
become too inhibited: a well-hit drive is one of the joys
of golf.

By all means spend plenty of time practising with the
driver: because of its straight face, it will tell you more
quickly than any other club about faults in your swing.

Chipping and pitching

These shots, which are normally played from close to
the green, are the most important of all for improving
your score. If you can chip or pitch with such accuracy
that you can get the ball into the hole in two shots from
a position off the green, you are well on the way to
returning consistently good scores. Golfers call this
"rolling three shots into two". On the other hand, if you
fluff your chips and pitches, and take four or five shots
from fifty yards out, your score will be bad no matter
how well you have played off the tee and up the fairway.

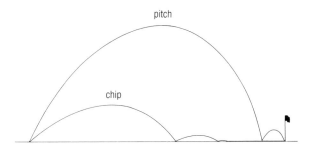

Figure 11 Trajectories of the chip and the pitch

Chipping

The chip is best thought of as a long putt, with the ball in the air for the first third or so of its course. Play a chip when there is no obstacle to go over between you and the hole. Hit the ball with anything from a 5- to an 8-iron, to produce a low-running shot. The condition of the ground will obviously affect the distance over which the ball will run when it lands. After you have been playing for a little while, one particular club will become your favourite for playing chip shots, and you will gain confidence from sticking to it.

Chipping tips

● Keep your weight on your left foot.

● Keep your hands ahead of the ball: they should be past the vertical line through the ball before the clubhead hits it.

● Keep your feet close together and adopt a slightly "open" stance.

● Use a short backswing — the most frequent cause of chipping failure is using too much backswing: there is then a tendency to decelerate the club just as it comes into the ball.

● Remember that although the chip is a delicate little shot, it must still be executed crisply.

● Take extra care when attempting to chip from a downhill lie: it is particularly difficult to lift the ball in this situation.

The address position for the chip shot: you should have your feet close together, and your stance should be slightly "open" so that you can swing your arms through easily.

There is no great backswing when chipping: the emphasis is on control and crispness.

Here, as the club is about to contact the ball, note that the hands are just slightly ahead of the clubhead. The weight remains on the left foot throughout the shot.

Pitching

The pitch shot is the one to play when you need to throw the ball up high over an obstacle such as a bunker, and then stop it quickly when it lands on the green. The stroke lifts the ball steeply, and gives it backspin. You use the wedge, or a 9-iron; both these clubs have a face which is inclined sharply backwards. As when chipping, keep your weight on your left foot, but this time take a longer backswing and "break the wrists" early rather than at the top of the backswing. Your hands should lead the clubhead on the downswing, and the clubhead should "slide" under the ball. The higher you want to throw the ball, the more "wristy" you should make the action — you will probably need quite a bit of practice to get the feel of it. Make sure you keep the clubhead going *down* as it hits the ball, otherwise you will play the most disastrous of short shots — the "thinned" wedge, in which the ball shoots low and far across the green because you have caught it with the front edge of the club.

No matter where the hole is on the green, until you have developed your golfing skills, you will find that it pays to aim for the centre of the green rather than for the flag. This will usually give you the greatest possible margin of safety, rather than risking disaster in the hope of spectacular success.

Putting

Putting is a game within the game. There are all kinds of putting styles which work, and if you are getting good results, stick with your own method. If not, here are a few tips:

● Make sure that the face of the putter travels in the direction that you want to hit the ball. You can check this by looking at your follow-through — the putter-head should continue along the line of the shot.

Concentrate on getting the length right for long putts such as this.

● Don't allow your wrists to play much part in the putting stroke, otherwise you will find it difficult to control the speed of the ball.

● Don't take too long a backswing on short putts, or you will decelerate as you come into the ball and fail to get a good strike.

● Keep the putterhead close to the ground. You will not be able to do this if you swing the putter straight back on the line of the shot — you will have to take it back on a slightly curved path: this is called swinging back "on the inside".

● Relax, but keep your wrists firm. You will never control a long putt by technique alone: you must have "feel".

● You should be aiming to get the ball into the hole in two putts at the most. Almost all three-putts come from errors of length, not line. There is an old but effective technique to use on long putts: imagine that a large barrel has been placed around the hole, and make your first putt with the aim of leaving the ball somewhere within its circumference.

● Keep your head still! Always!

Dealing with problems

Bunker play

Bunker shots terrify most beginners more than any other shot in golf, and many otherwise good rounds come to grief in the sand. As a novice, your first priority must be to get *out* — don't try anything spectacular. Most bunker shots are played from a greenside bunker, where the ball is lying on top of the sand; these shots do not have to be hit very hard.

This is the only shot where you set everything up to play a deliberate slice — take an "open" stance, but turn your hips and shoulders to a point left of the hole as well. Position yourself so that the ball is well forward in relation to your feet.

The club to use is your pitching wedge or a sand wedge if you have one. "Open" the face of the club (see panel on page 48). Take a fairly full backswing using your hands and arms rather than your shoulders, and swing gently through the sand beneath the ball. Concentrate on a relaxed, evenly-paced swing and follow-through. You should feel as though you are swinging your hands and arms gently through on the chosen line, flopping the ball out high on a cushion of sand. You will need to get the "feel" of the shot before you can play it with consistency.

"Opening" the clubface

For the majority of shots, you are trying to hit the ball with the clubhead square-on. Sometimes, however, it is useful to turn the club in your hands so that the face points more to the right than your shoulders. This is called "opening" the clubface. Hitting the ball with the clubface "open" produces a slice, which you must allow for.

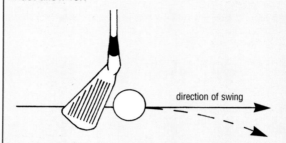

direction of swing

Figure 12 Play bunker shots with an "open" clubface which can slide through the sand under the ball.

It is helpful to see all your shots in your mind's eye before you play them, and this applies most of all to the bunker shot. What you are trying to do is to move the ball out of the bunker on a cushion of sand; the club-head enters the sand a few inches behind the ball and emerges about the same distance in front of it. This is often called a "poached-egg" shot — the ball is the yolk and the surrounding sand the white. Another trick is to imagine that the ball is lying on a banknote. Play the shot as if you are trying to deposit both note and ball together gently onto the green.

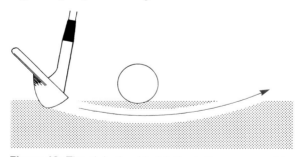

Figure 13 The club should pick the ball up on a cushion of sand.

As your game develops, you will be able to vary the distance that you hit bunker shots by changing the amount of sand you take, but your first priority must be to develop a shot which will always get you out!

The address position for the standard bunker shot is unusual, because you are about to play a deliberate slice! The ball is well forward in relation to your feet, and your hips and shoulders are pointing left of the hole.

Take an easy, fairly long backswing, keeping your eye on the point in the sand behind the ball where you plan to make contact.

The ball is "flopped out" on a cushion of sand: you cut across and under the ball.

Keep the club moving through the sand and into a full, rhythmical follow-through. Don't look up until the ball is safely out of the bunker.

Rules in the bunker

You must not let your club touch the sand before you swing it when playing a bunker shot — there is a two-stroke penalty for doing so.

You are not allowed to move loose impediments in bunkers or other hazards as you can elsewhere on the course. However, most golf clubs have a local rule which allows you to remove stones — check this. After every visit to a bunker, you should always rake over any footprints or hollows you have made.

Ball out of bounds or lost

If you hit your ball out of bounds, or you cannot find it, you must play again from the place where you hit your last shot. You are also penalised one stroke. For example, if you hit a bad tee shot into deep rough and cannot find your ball, you must return to the teeing ground, from where you will be hitting your *third* shot for that hole.

When you make a strike which you think has sent your ball out of bounds, or it has disappeared into very bad rough, it is often best to hit another ball before going off to search for the first one. You should declare that this is a "provisional" ball if that is what you intend. You can then continue to play with this "provisional" ball if your fears about the first are correct, otherwise you can simply pick it up. You *must* play your first ball if you find it in bounds — however horrific its position! Naturally, if you continue to play the provisional ball, you will incur the penalty described above.

When from the tee you are aiming for a narrow fairway, use a 3-wood or a 4-wood to increase your chance of hitting the ball straight. Unless you hit the ball perfectly with the driver, you may well get the ball just as far anyway. It is always worth thinking before you take out your driver — you cannot possibly score well if you are regularly in trouble off the tee.

Dropping or moving the ball

If your ball ends up in casual water, on ground under repair, or in a hole made by a burrowing animal, you are allowed to pick it up and drop it elsewhere without penalty. This process is called "taking relief". To drop your ball, you must find the nearest point to your ball where the ground is not affected and which is not nearer to the hole than its original lie (the "nearest point of relief"). Hold the ball at arm's length and drop it so that it lands within one club-length of the nearest point of relief.

If your ball is lying in casual water on the green, or there is casual water on the line of your putt, you may place the ball at the nearest position which affords relief and is not nearer the hole.

Trees are normally "part of the course", so you just have to make the best of things if your lie is uncomfortably close to one. However, a common local rule protects certain young trees by allowing you a "free drop".

Ball "plugged"

When the ground is wet, your ball may well bury itself in the ground when it lands. This is called being "plugged". If this happens in a "closely-mown" area, even where this may be no more than a path through the rough, you are allowed to pick the ball up, clean it, and drop it as near to its original position as possible, provided that it is then no nearer to the hole than its original lie. There is no penalty if you "lift and drop" like this in an area which is closely-mown, but if you do it anywhere else, you are penalised one stroke.

Cleaning your ball

The green is the only place where you are allowed to pick up your ball simply in order to clean it during play. The correct way to do this is to mark its position by placing a coin or a special marker immediately behind the ball before you lift it. Always replace the ball *before* you pick up the marker.

Impediments and obstructions

What do you do if your ball ends up against a snail or a cigarette packet, or settles under a bench?

Loose impediments are natural objects, such as stones, leaves, twigs, insects, or even dung, which are not fixed or growing from the ground. Snails come into this category. You are allowed to move them out of your way without penalty, except in a hazard. Always take care when removing loose impediments – there is a one-stroke penalty if your ball moves too!

Movable obstructions are artificial objects such as gardening tools, bottles or cigarette packets. These may be removed without penalty, so pick up the cigarette packet and play on. If your ball is resting on the obstruction, you are even allowed to pick it up, remove the offending article, and replace the ball without penalty.

Immovable obstructions are fixed artificial objects such as buildings, bridges and water tanks. If your ball lies so close to one of these that you are unable to take your stance or to swing at the ball, you may drop it at the closest point on the course which allows this and is not nearer to the hole. In this case there is no penalty. Take care, however: many permanent constructions are declared to be "part of the course", in which case you simply have to make the best of the position you have got yourself into. Check the local rules when you first play a new course.

A bench is an immovable obstruction if it is cemented into the ground; if you can shift it, then treat it as a movable obstruction.

The definitions given here are a general guide for newcomers to the game. The *Rules of Golf* define procedures very precisely, and when you begin to play serious competitive golf, you will gradually learn more and more of the details.

Striking the flagstick

If you make a stroke from the *putting green* which touches the flagstick, you are either penalised two strokes (in strokeplay) or lose the hole (in matchplay).

If your ball touches the flagstick after a stroke from a lie which is *not on the green*, then there is no penalty, provided there is not a caddie or anyone else attending the flag. If the flag is attended, the penalty for touching it is the same as if you hit it with a stroke from the green.

If you are having problems in this area, develop the habit of removing the flagstick as soon as you think you might hit it, and indicate clearly whether or not you want it removed when playing approach shots from further away.

Iain has wisely decided to have the flagstick attended for this long putt.

Course management

"Course management" is the modern term for "thinking your way" around a golf course. Work out tactics, not just at the beginning of each hole, but for each shot as the hole unfolds. For example:

● Do you need to use your driver for your tee-shot on every par-four hole? Probably not! Often a 3-wood or even an iron will pay better dividends on certain holes, particularly where there is a "dog-leg" in a narrow fairway.

● If you have played a reasonable tee shot, but still cannot be sure of reaching the green with one more stroke, what about playing your favourite 6-iron and following it with an 8-iron to the green? Mightn't this be a better option than playing a wood, which you know would almost certainly leave you short of the green with your very best shot, and lead to a lost ball with your worst?

● As a novice, your biggest problem will be to avoid complete disasters — scores of six turning into nines and tens. Accept your bad shots and try to recover; when in trouble, your priority should be to get back onto the fairway with the next shot, even if it means getting no nearer the hole. When your ball is in a bunker, you must get it out: you have in all probability lost a shot — do not let it become two or three in a red mist of fury or through misplaced optimism!

Matchplay strategy

In matchplay, a whole new range of calculations comes into play. If your opponent is in trouble, you will do well to play sensibly safe yourself. If he is going well, don't throw holes at him by playing wildly optimistic shots: make him work to win each hole. If you are a beginner, your handicap will probably give you shots at a number of holes. Use them to their full advantage: they are precious.

9

Etiquette

The basis of etiquette on the golf course is common sense and courtesy:

● Leave the course in the condition in which you found it — replace any divots you have made, repair your pitch marks on the green, and smooth over your footprints in bunkers.

*You can't avoid disturbing the sand when playing a bunker shot (**above**), but you should always smooth it out again afterwards (**below**). On most courses rakes are provided for this.*

- Be aware of other people on the course, both in front of you and behind you.

- Three- or four-ball matches should always let two-ball ones pass them.

- Let other players through if you are searching for a lost ball.

Slow play is the greatest source of annoyance in modern golf. In this one respect, professional golf often sets the worst possible example. Do not imitate the television performance of professionals on greens. Remember that they are playing for many thousands of pounds, on a different set of greens every week. Moreover, many professionals would normally prefer to play quickly: typical are Sandy Lyle and Ian Woosnam, who will be round in two-and-a-half hours when they are not impeded by matches in front.

You can also save time between shots:

- When you get your putter out, don't leave your bag at the front of the green and then go back to fetch it once you have finished the hole — put it on a direct line to the next tee.

- Think about your shot as your partner plays, and be ready when it is your turn to play, with your club selected.

- Mark your scorecard when your partner is playing from the tee on the next hole — don't hang about in the middle of the green and keep others waiting behind you.

A modern clubhouse in an attractive Pennine setting.

10
Joining a golf club

As your game improves, you will want to join a golf club and get the benefits of club facilities and regular competitions. Make enquiries as soon as you have decided that this is a game for you. Some clubs have an active junior section, while others are not quite so encouraging. Situations vary considerably in different parts of the British Isles and in other countries, but in most districts you will find there is a waiting list; often a considerable time will elapse before you can be considered for membership.

If you're lucky, there may be a public or municipal club where you will be able to play — particularly if you are prepared to turn out early in the morning, or during the middle of the week.

Develop your golf; get an official handicap if you possibly can, and set about reducing it. Most clubs will be more impressed by golfing prowess and enthusiasm than other qualities: rightly, for they are primarily *golf*, not social, clubs.

Most clubs have a pro shop — sometimes much bigger than this one — where you can get good advice as well as new equipment.

11
Warm-up exercises

Despite their skills and general fitness, professional golfers would not think of beginning a round without warming up first. You should develop your own small ritual for this. Hit a few balls in the practice net if there is one. Practise a few putts, but do not spend too long on the practice green expending the concentration you will need on the course. Particularly if you are past impetuous youth, you should warm up the golfing muscles, to ensure that your first swing is not traumatic. Whirl your arms a little and bend your knees gently. It is particularly important to warm up the big muscles in the shoulders and back before you play. Try the exercise shown here.

Pass a club behind your back as shown here, and practise a few gentle shoulder-turns against the resistance of the club. This is a useful exercise for warming up the shoulder and back muscles.

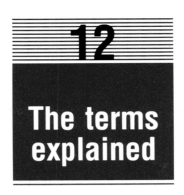

The terms explained

Some of these entries explain golfing expressions used in this book which are not covered in other chapters. Other entries explain terms which you may come across in other books or which you may hear on the television or on the golf course.

When explaining terms which describe the flight of the ball, we assume that a right-hander is playing. If you are a left-hander, simply read left for right and vice versa.

Borrow When putting, the amount you aim off the direct line from ball to hole in order to allow for the contours of the green is called *borrow*.

Caddie An attendant who carries a player's clubs. A luxury when taking up the game!

Draw A type of shot in which the ball curves slightly from right to left in its flight. A draw is made with the clubface slightly closed, and is a mild form of hook; with practice you can play a draw purposely: for example, to bend a shot round a tree.

Divot A small clod of earth or turf scooped out when the club hits the ground beneath the ball. Good golfers *always* replace their divots (see photos overleaf).

Fade A type of shot in which the ball curves slightly from left to right in its flight. A fade is made with the clubface slightly open, and is a mild form of slice. Like the draw, a fade can be played deliberately in order to bend the ball around an obstacle.

Fluffing A type of mishit in which the club hits the ground before the ball, taking the power out of the shot.

Fore! The traditional word to use to warn other people on the course that they are in danger from a flying ball. Don't be afraid to shout it loudly — it could save someone from a nasty injury.

Take care always to replace your divots ...

Hole The actual hole on the putting green must be of the dimensions specified in the rules — 4.25 inches (108 mm) in diameter and at least 4 inches (100 mm) deep.

Honour When two or more players are playing together, the order in which they play their tee shots is decided by the scores they made on the previous hole. The player or team who made the lowest score has the *honour* and must play first.

Lie The position where the ball ends up after any shot is called its *lie*. A lie is often described according to how difficult to play it makes the ball — the two extremes being a *good lie* and an *unplayable lie*.

... and to tread them in firmly.

Loft Either the height of the ball's flight or the angle of the clubface. Because their faces are inclined quite steeply backwards, the shorter irons are often called *lofted clubs*.

Rub of the green Accidental interference with a *moving* ball by anybody or anything that is not part of your particular game. It may mean good or bad luck for the player, and no penalty is involved.

Scratch player A golfer whose handicap is zero (see chapter 6).

Shanking A type of mishit in which the heel of the club, rather than the clubface, connects with the ball. The ball spins away to the right.

Toeing A type of mishit in which the toe of the club, rather than the clubface, connects with the ball. In extreme cases the ball can shoot off at right angles.

Topping Hitting the top half of the ball with the bottom edge of the clubface. This sort of mishit forces the ball hard into the ground.

Pitch marks — the dents caused by pitched shots landing on the green — should always be carefully repaired.

Useful addresses

Great Britain

The Royal and Ancient Golf Club of St Andrews
St Andrews
Fife
Scotland
KY16 9JD

Professional Golfers Association
Apollo House
The Belfry
Wishaw
Sutton Coldfield
West Midlands
B76 9PT

Overseas

Australian Golf Union
3 Bowen Crescent (9th Floor)
Melbourne 3004
Australia

Royal Canadian Golf Association
Golf House
RR No 2
Oakville
Ontario
Canada
L6J 4Z3

New Zealand Golf Association
Dominion Sports House
Mercer Street
PO Box 11842
Wellington
New Zealand

United States Golf Association
Golf House
Liberty Corner Road
Far Hills
New Jersey 07931
USA

International

The Royal and Ancient Golf Club of St Andrews
St Andrews
Fife
KY16 9YD
United Kingdom

United States Golf Association
Golf House
Liberty Corner Road
Far Hills
New Jersey 07931
USA